Ages 3+

WONDER MAGIC DRAWING

Practice Workbook For Preschoolers

Vanishing Ink | Reusable in 15 minutes | Thick Paper

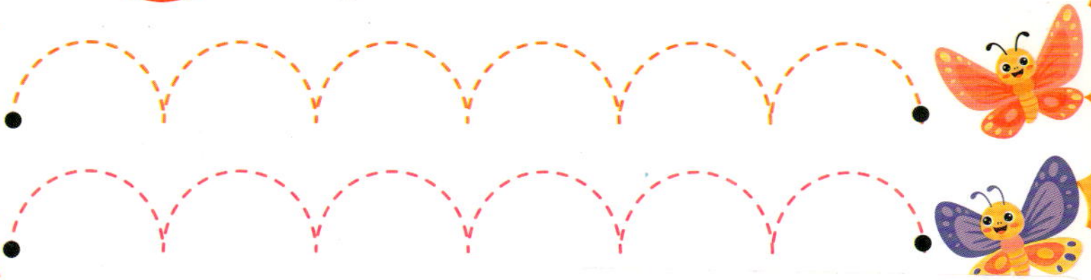

Wonder House

Includes penholder, gripper and refills

Note 1:

Extra-thick paper, no curling, the product uses the groove design to constrain the user's writing habits, use the special faded stylus pen, the writing will disappear automatically after writing, the basic handwriting is gone, the front handwriting has disappeared, no need to wait, Reusable, environmentally friendly and energy efficient.

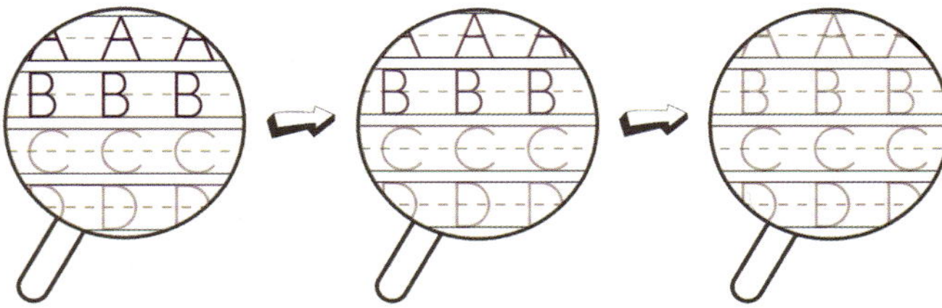

Note2:

This product is forbidden to wipe with force. Do not wipe with a damp cloth. Please keep it in a dry and ventilated place.

Note3:

1. Only use the special pen core for the product to write, the handwriting will disappear.
2. When the special pen core is in use, the ink may be clogged. Use the pen tip to lightly write several times on ordinary white paper, After the ink is smooth, then start the practice.
3. As the ink is specially processed, the handwriting will disappear after writing. Please do not use it for daily writing, record important information and sign documents, so as to avoid unnecessary losses to you.

Lines

Puzzle Games

Draw in the grid.

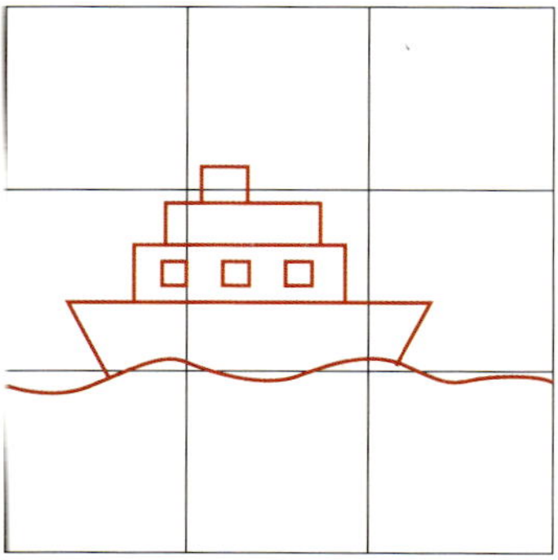

Find the correct shadow.

(1)

(2)

(3)

Shapes

Read and Draw

Draw a butterfly.

Butterfly, butterfly
Fly in the sky.
Butterfly, butterfly
Flies so high.

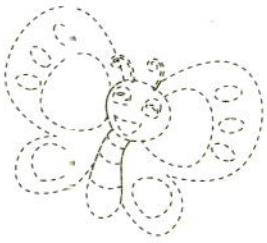

Shapes

Puzzle Games

Draw in the grid.

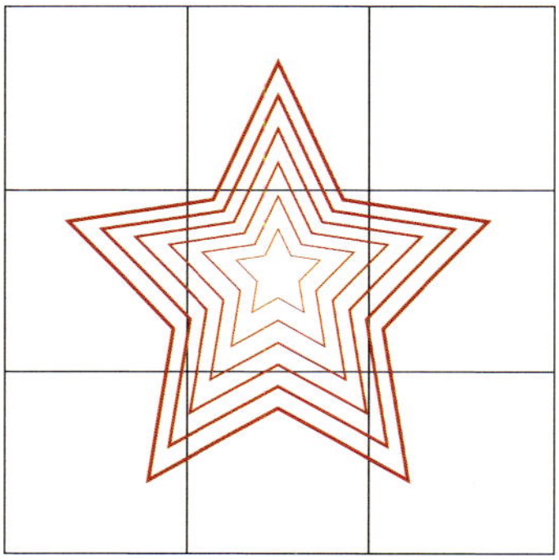

Find the correct shadow.

(1)

(2)

(3)

Vegetables

Puzzle Game

Arrange the pictures on the right by placing correct numbers.

Fruits

Find two differences

Animals

Painting and Drawing

Can you draw this painting?

Happy Holiday

Fun Sports

How many sports do you see?

Flowers

Identify Differences

GOOD POSTURE

1.Both feet on the floor
2.Elbows off edge of desk
3.Sit back in the chair
4.Shoulders slightly forward
5.Proper desk height

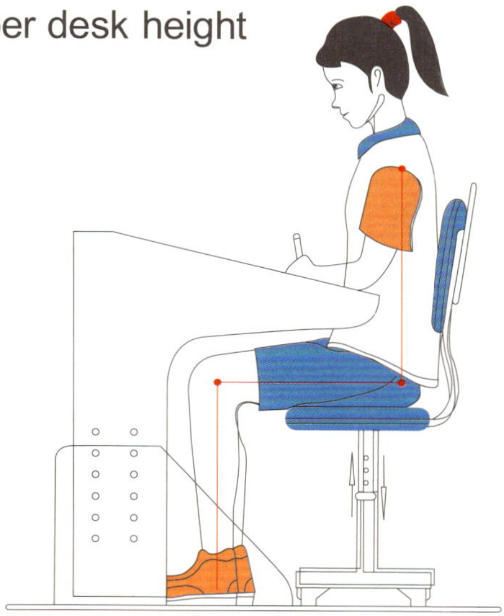

GOOD HANDWRITING

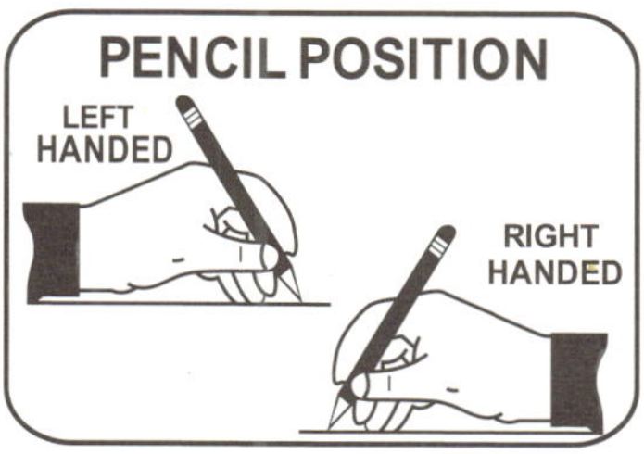

WONDER MAGIC DRAWING

Practice Workbook For Preschoolers

Get ready to embark on a drawing journey like no other! This interactive book for beginners with vanishing ink will inspire children to practice drawing repeatedly. The book allows beginners to enhance their drawing skills by following the grooves to form perfect images.

Let the interactive book guide you to draw confidently and have fun!

Titles in the series

Wonder House

Wonder House Books is an imprint of Prakash Books

UK £ 1.99 CAN $ 4.99 US $ 2.99

ISBN: 978-93-6214-378-5

9 789362 143785

Wonder House

MRP

www.wonderhousebooks.com • 00005900

wonderhousebooks wonderhousebooks wonderhousebook